SALISBURY

THROUGH TIME

Carol Dixon-Smith &
Catherine Essenhigh

AMBERLEY

Acknowledgements

We, the authors, would like to thank all who aided and abetted us in our endeavours to produce this book, particularly the staff in Salisbury Library, Five Rivers Recruitment, Mr Craig Ancliff, and Mrs Kate Beckett from Friends of Salisbury Cathedral.

The greatest thanks, however, must go to our long-suffering families for their support, encouragement, taxi services, and numerous pots of tea. They were invaluable.

All photographs, postcards, prints, and illustrations are from the authors' private collections except as indicated here:

2013 Rifles Regiment Parade, www.craig-photos.me.uk
St Andrew Statue: Richard Avery, Public Domain, commons.wikimedia.org/w/index.php?curid=10626476
Steam Laundry: Chris Talbot www.geograph.org.uk/profile/1249 Creative Commons 2.0 license

For William Edwin
the circle is complete

First published 2016

Amberley Publishing
The Hill, Stroud, Gloucestershire, GL5 4EP
www.amberley-books.com

Copyright © Carol Dixon-Smith & Catherine
Essenhigh, 2016

The right of Carol Dixon-Smith & Catherine Essenhigh
to be identified as the Authors of this work has been
asserted in accordance with the Copyrights, Designs and
Patents Act 1988.

ISBN 978 1 4456 5799 8 (print)
ISBN 978 1 4456 5800 1 (ebook)

British Library Cataloguing in Publication Data.
A catalogue record for this book is available from the
British Library.

Origination by Amberley Publishing.
Printed in Great Britain.

Introduction

Upon approach to the city from the north, crossing the lines of two Roman roads, the traveller is immediately drawn to the impressive ramparts of an Iron Age fortification, within which lie the remains of the first Salisbury Cathedral. You have reached Old Sarum. This first cathedral was badly sited, and only its foundations remain today.

Travelling on, as you peak the hill by Old Sarum, the renowned spire of the New Sarum cathedral sits nestled in the modern city. In April 1220, clerics from that first cathedral witnessed the laying of the foundation stones of the new cathedral, dedicated to the Blessed Virgin Mary. It is the home of one of the four surviving original Magna Carta manuscripts, and has the tallest spire in the United Kingdom. In the evenings, the red beacon topping the spire acts to keep aircraft safe, and is like a guide to visitors to Salisbury, a small city of around 45,000 souls set in the verdant and archaeologically rich landscape of south Wiltshire.

The first part of the cathedral to be finished was Trinity Chapel, which today houses the 'Prisoners of Conscience' window. It was nearly forty years before the main body of the cathedral was completed, and during that time the town grew. Master craftsmen, labourers, suppliers and their families all added to the burgeoning settlement and to its economy. Salisbury is essentially a medieval town.

It was in 1227 that Salisbury was granted its first royal charter, which gave permission for a market each Tuesday. In 1361, after a dispute, a second market was granted for each Saturday. Various fairs had been granted over the decades, but the grant in 1271 permitted a fair in October. In 1612, James I granted an Act of Incorporation enabling the city elders to move away from the dominance of the cathedral and govern more independently.

Given the farming methods of the day, with extensive sheep grazing on the downs and arable land, the inevitable by-product was wool. Initially, Salisbury was selling raw wool. Both men and women were involved in the trade, as evidenced in 1275 when fifteen were caught trying to evade export restrictions. By the fifteenth century, Salisbury was one of the more important cloth-making centres in England, exporting its cloth to mainland Europe and around the Mediterranean. Several of the buildings remaining from that period were built by these merchants.

For a number of reasons, Salisbury did not expand with the advent of the railways in the way that many other cities did. While businessmen at the time may have rued that, it has contributed to leaving much of the city's heritage intact.

Salisbury, like many other towns, had benefactors who gave money or buildings for a variety of causes, from schools to almshouses, hospitals to workhouses. Now in the twenty-first century, we can see the fruits of the past and experience history at work, and not only in the buildings. For example, the Charter Market is still held every Tuesday and Saturday, except in October when the Charter Fair is held on the third Tuesday.

Many visitors to the city regard it as the epitome of a traditional English settlement, yet just like the rest of the United Kingdom, Salisbury has altered over the centuries as a consequence of social, economic and political change. While the cathedral clearly dominates the landscape, what is fascinating is not how much Salisbury has changed and grown around it, nor what has been lost, but how much of the city's past remains alive. The centre is still laid in its medieval grid pattern, each block known as a chequer and each with its own distinct name. Each century has left its mark, from houses and churches, pubs, shops, and street names; it is impossible to avoid, and hard to ignore. The city's unique ability to interweave its history with the modern and technological ensures its rich cultural heritage is available and on show to all, even those not looking for it – it is the only place where you go to the cinema in a medieval hall!

The advent of photography has proved to be a godsend to those who are interested in the past. The Victorians and Edwardians embraced the new technology with zeal and left us a treasure trove of imagery. Salisbury was no exception to this, as postcard companies and photographers such as Francis Frith, Raphael Tuck and Southampton-based F. G. O. Stuart covered the length and breadth of the United Kingdom. We are however deeply indebted to Salisbury photographers such as Witcomb, Messer, Juke and Futcher (father and son), and as time has moved on from them, each generation has added more, thus giving us the opportunity to chart visually the changes that have taken place.

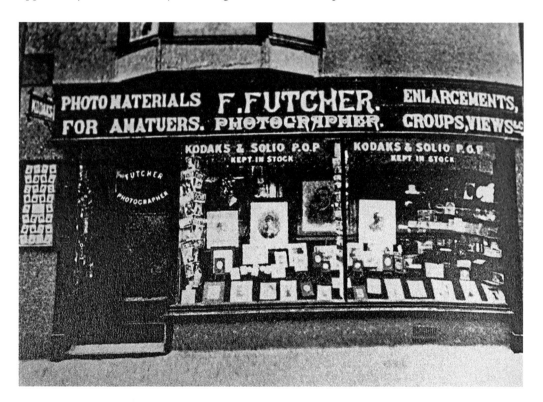

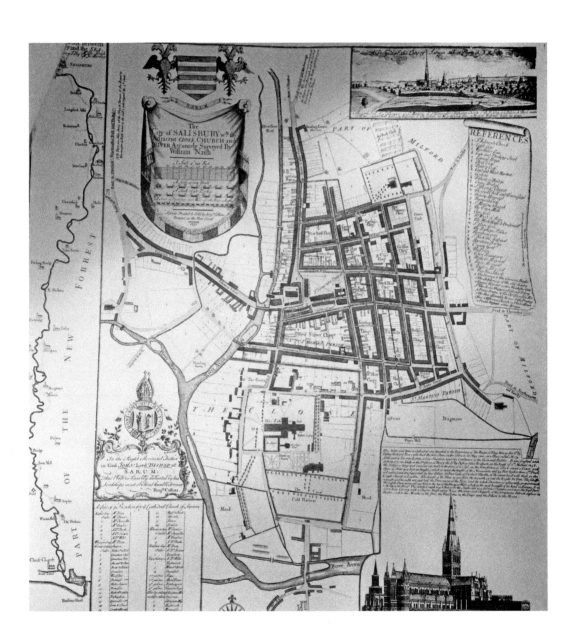

5

General View of Excavations at Old Sarum

Old Sarum

Excavations of the post-Conquest castle and its associated buildings at Old Sarum. The stone structures were built between the twelfth and early thirteenth centuries, almost certainly replacing earlier wooden buildings. This view shows the corner of St Nicholas' Chapel at the right. The taller of the extant walls, left of the chapel, were part of the courtyard house. The circular feature in front of the buildings in the recent picture is a well.

Old Sarum, St Nicholas Chapel
In the foreground is the chapel with the guardroom to its right; the castle keep is in the background left. It was not the only chapel in the castle. An order of 1246 stated that a lamp must be kept burning day and night in the chapel of St Nicholas. In 1315, money was granted to repair the chapel and other parts of the castle that had been damaged in a storm.

Old Castle Inn

The Old Castle Inn was situated opposite Old Sarum and on the main northern route out of the city, now the A345. It was well positioned for passing trade and tourists visiting Old Sarum, and is now a Harvester Inn. The central part of the inn was built in the latter half of the sixteenth century and it has eighteenth-century extensions.

Victoria Park, Salisbury

Victoria Park
The park was laid out in 1887 to mark Queen Victoria's Golden Jubilee. The bandstand is now long gone, but it remains an important community asset with facilities such as tennis courts and a tennis club, bowling green football pitch and a children's playground. It was home to Salisbury Football Club until it moved to the purpose-built Raymond McEnhill Stadium at Old Sarum in 1997.

Castle Street
The New Picturedrome & Theatre was opened in 1910, part of Albany Ward's circuit and he is listed as managing director. It was remodelled in 1913 and was mainly used for live shows, though it showed films at other times. It was taken over by Provincial Cinematograph Theatres, and then in 1929 by the Gaumont chain, who closed New Theatre in April 1932 with the film *Mother & Son* starring Clara Kimball Young.

Post Office
The post office was built in 1905 at the corner of Castle Street and Chipper Lane. It is now closed having been relocated in 2016 to the corner of Endless Street and Winchester Street.

Brewery

Tesco now stands on the Castle Street site. Kelly's Directory of 1867 records George Pain & Son here: 'brewers, maltsters, hop, spirit & coal merchants, Castle street brewery'. Clearly not simply brewing and malting, but also merchants selling a small range of goods.

Cheesemarket and Maidenhead Inn

The inn was run by Joseph Hibberd with his wife Jane, who continued as proprietor after his death in 1827. The inn was replaced in 1858 by the Market House. The library now stands on the site but Market House is remembered in the naming of Market Walk, which runs to the south side of the library.

Market House

Market House was built in 1858. In 1859, a branch line running to it from the railway was opened, which proved important in maintaining the success of the market. This continued in use until the mid-1960s. The branch line and market have long gone, but the façade of the Market House was saved and incorporated into the new library, opened in 1975.

Market Place. Salisbury.

Market Place Corner

Market Place Corner is pictured in the early twentieth century showing Mairs & Sons, and the International Stores on the corner opposite Blue Boar Row. The corner building, which once housed the Girl Guides retail outlet upstairs, is now under renovation. There are plans for the upper part to become residential units and the ground floor is Allum & Sidaway Jewellers, who are moving from a shop opposite on Queen Street.

Blue Boar Row

Facing the Market Place, on the north side, is Blue Boar Row. Its name comes from an inn that stood on the site from at least the fifteenth century and remained in use until the early nineteenth century. Reference to building a house 'within the Boor' in 1444 may refer to the timber-framed hall at the back of the site (currently Debenhams).

Queen Street

This image shows Queen Street fronting the Market Square, showing the Old Bank in the left foreground and Turkish Baths to the left of the Guildhall. In the 1880s the proprietor of the Turkish Baths was J. M. Jenkins. The street comprises one full side of the Cross Keys Chequer and was the birthplace of Henry Fawcett (1833–84), the blind Postmaster General. By 1898, Salisbury Old Bank had merged with Wilts & Dorset Banking Ltd and had John and William Pinckney in charge.

John A'Port's House
The building in Queen Street is erroneously attributed to John A'Port but was actually that of the merchant William Russel. Built around 1306–14, it is possibly the oldest timber-framed building surviving in the city. Now Crew Clothing, the premises were formerly Watson's China Shop, a local family firm established in 1834, which sadly closed in 2008.

Council House, Salisbury

The Elizabethan Council House was secular, and the bishop had his own Guildhall, which stood behind. After 1612, the power of the bishop over the city weakened as James I granted Salisbury a Charter of Incorporation. The present Guildhall was built in the 1780s after the old one was damaged by fire. Both it and Bishop's Guildhall were pulled down afterwards.

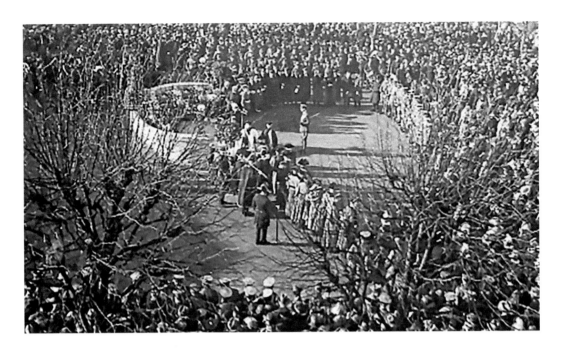

Salisbury War Memorial 1922

The Salisbury War Memorial was unveiled by Lt Thomas Edward Adlam VC (Victoria Cross) on 12 February 1922. Born in 1893, Adlam lived in Waterloo Gardens; he went to Bishop Wordsworth's School, the grammar school for boys in Salisbury. Before the war, Adlam was in the Territorial Force (TF), forerunner to the Territorial Army (TA), and in 1915 was commissioned into the Bedfordshire Regiment. He then trained as a bombing officer, winning his VC on 27 September 1916 at Thiepval, France.

Regiments on Parade

On 3 December 1947, the Wiltshire Regiment was awarded the Freedom of Salisbury, and after the ceremony, held in the Market Square, the Regiment paraded through the town. Although amalgamations mean that there is no longer a distinct Wiltshire Regiment, it lives on through the Rifles Regiment. On 9 December 2013, 4th Battalion Rifles marked their return from Afghanistan by exercising their Freedom of Salisbury and paraded through the city after a medal ceremony in the barracks.

Ox Row

The images shows the City Arms as it was; the name can be seen standing out below the bay window. The address was simply 'Market Place' in 1867 when Edward William Casey was the landlord. Signwriting in the bay window, intended to be read from outside, advertises a 'BILLIARD SALON AND LOUNGE', so the pub was offering entertainment as well as drink. It is now the Ox Row Inn (Ox Row), with the more modern development of an outdoor drinking and eating area to the front.

Minster Street

The image shows Minster Street looking south on the print, with the Haunch of Venison pub on the right and Carters jewellers just before it. Buildings here range from the fifteenth through to the nineteenth century, either in whole or in part. Until the 1850s, a water channel ran along the side of the street. These drains were a health hazard and were covered over in the 1850s. Below is a modern view from the opposite direction.

Poultry Cross

A pre-1852 view of the Poultry Cross before restoration and the addition of the upper buttresses and pinnacle. The proposal to alter the upper part of the Poultry Cross was first published in 1834 by Peter Hall and designed by Owen Carter, but the work was not executed until 1852.

Poultry Cross and Butcher's Row

A view of the Poultry Cross looking down towards Butcher's Row. Oliver's shoe warehouse is on the right, with Charles Haskins, clothier and china and glass dealer, opposite. Note the contrast between the two young men road sweeping on the right and the clearly carefully posed, well-dressed young boys around the Poultry Cross.

Silver Street

Looking along Silver Street towards the Poultry Cross and Butchers' Row. Charles Rawlings' outfitters is to the left and a passageway to St Thomas' churchyard, still extant, is just beyond the shop to the right of Rawlings' stores.

Corner of High Street and Silver Street

The late nineteenth century saw a rapid expansion of pharmacies, including William Day's Southern Drug Co. that started in the 1890s. He had sixty branches throughout London and the south of England by 1900 when he was bought out by Jesse Boot, founder of the modern-day Boots company. The building is now occupied by a fast-food retailer.

St Thomas' Church

Built in 1240 as a chapel of ease for the cathedral, the church of St Thomas à Becket was the first active place of worship in New Sarum. A restored doom painting above the chancel arch, painted in 1475 in thanksgiving for the safe return of a pilgrim, is worthy of note, as are other late fifteenth-century wall paintings in the church.

St Thomas' Churchyard Salisbury

A little-changed view of the churchyard. It shows the rear views of shops and houses that front Minster Street and Silver Street. The churchyard itself is an oasis on busy days, with benches for those who might want to sit in calm reflection away from the clamour of the shoppers and cars.

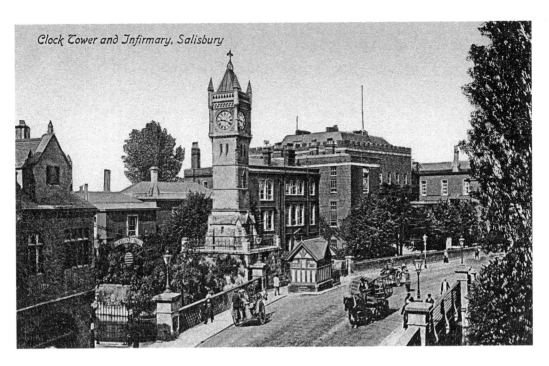

Clock Tower and Infirmary, Salisbury

Clock Tower and Infirmary

Erected in 1767 with voluntary subscriptions, Salisbury Infirmary has been converted into luxury apartments. The clock tower to the left was constructed in 1892–93. It sits atop a much older 'lock-up' – a remnant of the County Gaol that is now long gone. Also long gone is the cabbies' rest room and the public conveniences that stood by the clock tower.

The County Hotel

With several names changes over the centuries, an inn has stood on this site since the fifteenth century. It was onced was called The Ram, but the name changed in 1528 to the King's Head. It was listed under that name in Kelly's 1889 Directory, but at some point the name changed to the County Hotel. In 2002, Wetherspoons, the new owners, changed it back to the King's Head.

Maundrell Hall and the Bridge
Named after one of Fisherton's
Protestant martyrs, Maundrell
Hall opened in 1880. It was for
non-denominational worship and
discussion, especially for the poor
who were not regular churchgoers.
Later buildings next to it included
the Star of Hope Temperance Hotel
and the Princess Christian Home
for Women. At the time of this
photograph, the hall houses the
Church of England Institute. There
are two American soldiers on the left
of the photo, so it has been taken
sometime after 1942.

Fisherton Street Methodist Church (United Reformed Church)

The congregation dates backs to the seventeenth century and to the Dissenter, John Strickland, who was ejected from St Edmund's in 1662. Services and meetings were held in a variety of locations until one location was settled upon – in Fisherton Street in 1878. The church was redeveloped in 1978, moving the sanctuary and creating a new hall and meeting spaces.

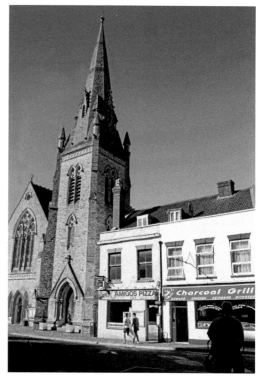

Clock Tower and Cabs
Showing the horse-drawn cab rank (the main cab rank is now in New Canal). The garden by the infirmary has long been replaced with shops, but the buildings opposite remain, though with a very different purpose now. What was the Star of Hope Temperance Hotel is now a fast-food outlet.

Fisherton Street Floods 1915
The autumn and winter of 1914/1915 had been bad, with floods in Salisbury and on Salisbury Plain. The jocularity of the soldier belies the fact that soldiers were living in huts in close quarters on the plain. The cold weather and flooding meant many suffered colds, flu and even meningitis, some of which proved deadly.

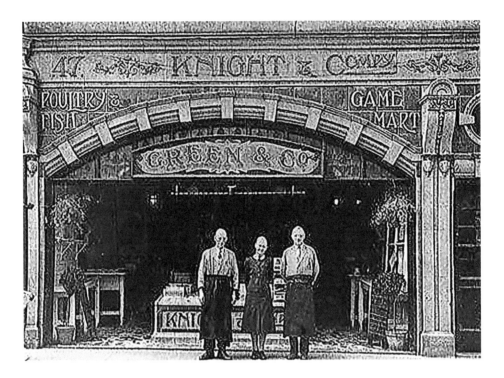

Knight & Co. Building

The Knight & Co. building is a good example of a turn-of-the-nineteenth-century tiled shop façade. Knight and Co. do not appear in the 1903 Kelly's Directory, but they were at this address by 1907. However, their stay was short-lived as it had become Green & Co. fishmongers by 1911. The façade was boarded over when it became unfashionable. Now uncovered, the consequent damage from the boarding can be seen.

Fisherton Street Picture House

The building remains connected to entertainment as it is now the home of Spire FM, the local radio station. Note the link in the radio station name to the cathedral which dominates the city. Sadly, the façade of the building was partly demolished.

Fisherton Street Cinema

In the late 1920s the Picture House was showing *The Loves of Carmen* with leading lady Delores Del Rio, leading man Victor McLaglen, and directed by Raoul Walsh. Multiyork furniture shop is now on the site.

The Railway Bridge

The railway bridge here is going over the top of Fisherton Street, with Dews Road and South Western Road towards the right under it. It was constructed in 1906 for the London and South Western Railway.

Railway Station
The railway station was built in 1902 and outwardly has changed little, apart from the motorised taxis. The earlier station of the 1850s still remains, to the east of the present building.

HQ 2nd Army Corps

Radnor House was built in 1818–22 as the central administration building of the county gaol. When the gaol was closed in 1870, and largely demolished, Radnor House was saved and became a private residence from 1875. HQ 2nd Army Corps (later HQ Southern Command), was housed there from 1901 until its demolition in 1959. The well-trained soldiers are observing cycle drill correctly, with both hands on the bars and pushing from their right-hand side!

Bemerton Village

Bemerton village, known as Lower Bemerton and part of Salisbury, has many modern additions, though much remains of the buildings seen in the older picture here. Once a separate village, it was a chapelry of Fugglestone St Peter until 1894, when it became a parish in its own right. It has three Anglican churches: St Andrew's (Norman and Middle Ages), St John's (1861 Gothic Revival) and St Michael's (1957).

Bemerton Church with Rectory
St Andrew's is an old church of flint with ashlar dressings. The poet and hymn writer George Herbert was priest here and lived in the rectory beside the church. He died in March 1633. Repairs and restorations were carried out throughout the eighteenth and nineteenth centuries.

Nurses Home

This was the Salisbury Institute for Trained Nurses, situated on the corner of Harcourt Terrace and Harcourt Bridge Road (now Mill Road). Having been a private institution, it was acquired by Salisbury Hospitals in the 1940s, fell out of use in the 1990s, and is now private housing with an attractive view of Queen Elizabeth Gardens opposite.

Crane Bridge

Providing a crossing over the River Avon, one arch on the north side (left in the picture), may be medieval; much of the rest is seventeenth and late nineteenth century. The bridge was widened in 1898 when the south side of it was rebuilt. It now carries traffic into the city.

Workhouse

This building was built on Crane Street in the fifteenth century for William Lightfoot, a wealthy clothier. It became the workhouse in 1638. From 1881, it has been used by the cathedral authorities as an administrative centre for the Diocese, and is called Church House. The building has been extended during different phases of its history.

High Street

This view shows the High Street from the New Canal corner looking down to the Close Gate. Salisbury is clearly a book-reading town; the directories show an abundance of booksellers, several of which were on the High Street. The shop on the corner of this picture is still a bookshop, at present Waterstones.

The Old George Hotel, Salisbury.

The Old George Inn

The Old George Inn was partly demolished in 1967. It is now occupied by Boston Tea Party and is a meeting place and haunt of Salisbury sixth-formers! It was probably the most important of Salisbury's medieval inns. The entrance to the Old George Mall was formed by the Inn's existing carriageway and part of the lower story.

OLD GEORGE MALL

The Old George Inn Garden
The garden disappeared under the Old George Mall Shopping Centre on the High Street when it was constructed in the 1960s.

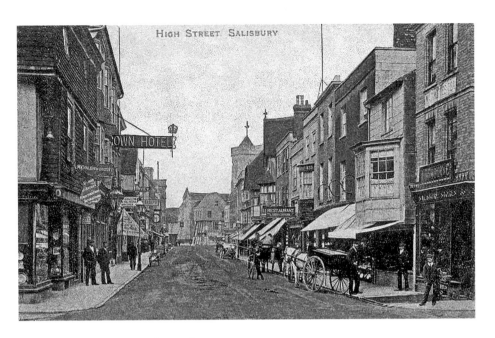

High Street (Towards St Thomas')
The image shows the shop of Mrs Alice Mary Goldsworthy, an antique furniture dealer, on the corner of High Street and Crane Street. The 1898 Kelly's Directory lists the business in her husband James' name as a cycle agent, but she was widowed in 1901, and by 1907 onwards it was being run by Alice as an antiques business, employing two of her daughters. It is now a charity shop. In the distance, the west front of St Thomas' Church can be seen.

High Street from Close Gate

Beach's Bookshop (now Prezzo) on the corner of High Street and Crane Street. The bookshop closed in the 1990s. The building was originally three single-gabled, jettied houses built in the fourteenth century, but had consisted of just one property for some time. Upstairs, some earlier wall painting has been uncovered and left for the patrons to view and enjoy.

Close Gate, Salisbury
Ap. 24 1905

Close Gate
Taken in 1905, beyond the gate on the left the sign of the Crown Hotel can just be seen. In Kelly's Directory of 1903 it was advertising itself as 'Crown Hotel; the nearest hotel to the Cathedral; quiet & comfortable accommodation (Thomas South, proprietor), wine & spirit merchant, and agent for Groves' famous Weymouth ales, High street & Crane street'.

College of Matrons

On the right by the Close Gate are the almshouses that were founded in 1683 by Seth Ward, then Bishop of Salisbury. Applicants to the College of Matrons had to fulfil certain conditions: 'Matrons shall be needy and deserving single women ... preference being given to widows and daughters of Ministers of the Church of England.' The college remains an almshouse with the same criteria for eligibility. Outwardly, the building is unaltered, ivy excepted; internal alterations to accommodate modern life have been made over the years.

West Front of Cathedral
Sheep grazing in the close is one way of keeping the grass short. This somewhat idyllic 'rural' scene is long gone, but most interesting in the view are the empty niches. The statuary we see today was installed by Sir George Gilbert Scott during his work on the cathedral in the 1870s.

Grammar School

Now called Wren Hall, it was remodelled in 1714 from part of Braybrook House (left of the picture), to form a school for the cathedral choristers. Braybrook House housed the Master, and dormitories were in the attic of Wren Hall. Choristers' Green, in front of Wren Hall, is so named because of its use by the boys of the choir. The hall has recently been used as an education centre for the cathedral.

Teacher Training College

The King's House in Salisbury Cathedral Close was a medieval building that in 1841 came into use as the Diocesan Training College for women wishing to enter teaching. After closure of the college in 1978, it became the home of the Salisbury and South Wilts Museum. Lauded by the writer Bill Bryson, it is home to the Pitt-Rivers collection and opened to complement the work of redeveloping the facilities at Stonehenge with an impressive new gallery.

Harnham Gate

The gateway via De Vaux Road into the Cathedral Close. In July 2016, an alleged drunk driver drove into the medieval gate. Although the fourteenth-century stonework was unharmed, the gates, belonging to restoration work of 1937, were badly damaged. It is now undergoing conservation and repair before it is put back; the keystone loosened in the impact has been repaired.

St Nicholas Hospital

An almshouse in Farnham, near Ayleswade Bridge. The hospital was founded in 1215 for 'the reception, care and maintenance of Christ's poor, sick and infirm', and continues to thrive to this day, with a mixed community of men and women. The 1805 print suggests a larger complex than we see today, however, significant modern additions to the rear have replaced the walls and buildings at the front, which have clearly been demolished.

Harnham Bridge

Also known as Ayleswade Bridge, Harnham Bridge was built around 1244 by Bishop Bingham, though much that can be seen now belongs to alterations made in 1774 to widen the bridge. Traffic lights now control the traffic rather than the policemen shepherding it!

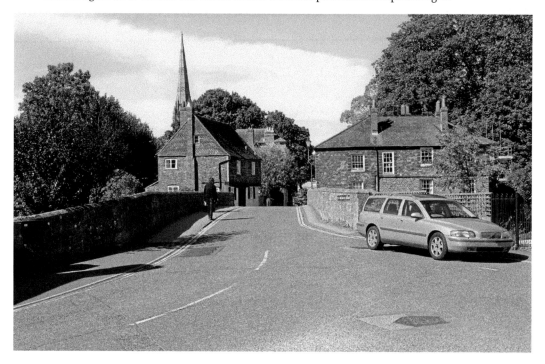

Harnham village

Showing the Rose and Crown pub and hotel, which is still operating. The thatched building opposite has clearly been replaced. A settlement has existed here since the Iron Age, and it is mentioned in the Domesday Book. An 1870 guide lists it as 'a tything and a chapelry in Britford parish'.

Rose and Crown Riverside

The 1937 visitors who sent this picture of the gardens at the rear of the Rose and Crown in Harnham have written: 'Beautiful gardens & white swans on the narrow river flowing by the garden, where they have white pigeons and lovely flowers. Back is much prettier than the front.' The writer is an unnamed guest.

Old Mill
Once one of Salisbury's fulling mills, the nineteenth-century picture shows it in a rather dilapidated state. There is some evidence it may also have functioned as a paper mill. Built around 1500, an external part of the mill was sketched by J. M. W. Turner during his early career, showing some of the attractive ashlar and flint stone construction.

De Vaux Road

Looking along to Harnham Gate, into the Cathedral Close. The single-story building on the right has served as one of the boarding houses for Leadenhall, a girls' prep school that amalgamated with the Salisbury Cathedral School in 2016.

North Walk in the Close
Running from St Ann's Gate to the West Walk, with an uninterrupted view of the north face of Salisbury Cathedral. The building opposite the post box has been, at different times, a family home, Salisbury Guide headquarters, cathedral offices, but now houses the Friends of the Cathedral. The post box is still *in situ* and in use.

Theological College

Salisbury has been an important centre for theological training since the early Middle Ages, and there has been a college here since the establishment of the cathedral. Eight of the college's students were killed in the Great War. Now it is home to Sarum College, an ecumenical study and research centre, carrying on the tradition of Christian education.

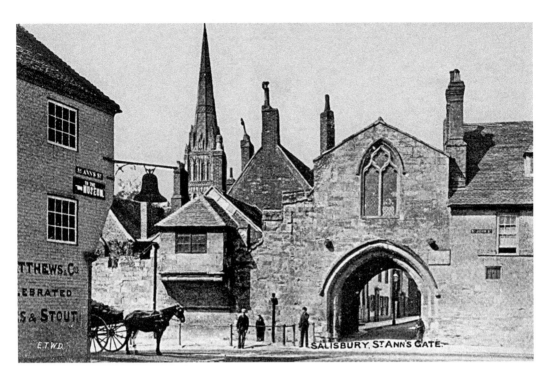

St Ann's Gate

Situated on Exeter Street is St Ann's Gate, also leading into the Cathedral Close. Note the museum sign indicating the route to the Blackmore Museum, later amalgamated with Salisbury and South Wilts Museum.

The White Hart Hotel

This is now part of the Mercure group. Traditionally, from the balcony of the hotel, each newly elected Member of Parliament (MP) sings in Wiltshire dialect, the song entitled 'The Vly [fly] be on the Turmut [turnip]'. The verse is: 'The vly, the vly, the vly be on the turmut,' 'Tis all me eye, for oi [I] to try, to keep vlies off them turmuts'.

St Ann Street
Falling within the parish of
St Martin, which pre-dates the
cathedral, St Ann Street was known
as St Martin's Street until the
sixteenth century. Although mostly
eighteenth-century buildings now,
parts are still much older. Joiners'
Hall is located here.

Blackmore Museum

The ebonised cases depicted and packed with artefacts are typically Victorian. The Blackmore Museum founded in 1864 by Dr W. Blackmore later amalgamated with the Salisbury and South Wilts Museum, had an ethnographic collection, which was formed of finds located in rubbish deposits, exposed when the city water channels were drained. Located in St Ann's Street it is now luxury flats and maisonettes. In 1981, the collection moved into the King's House, in the Close, becoming the Salisbury, South Wilts and Blackmore Museum.

Salisbury, Joiners Hall.

Joiners' Hall

This belonged to the Guild of Craftsmen and was probably built around 1612. The hall is in St Ann's Street and was regarded by Nikolaus Pevsner as the best timber-framed house in Salisbury. Carved below the middle bays are some unusual figures with male heads. The detail of the heads suggests they may have been caricatures of real men, with their attachment to exaggerated female bodies possibly intended as an insult.

Clock Factory Fire, 1909

Owned by the London clockmakers Williamson & Son, the English Clock Factory was a very successful firm, employing several hundred people locally. The 1909 fire destroyed it and, although there were no injuries, it was a local disaster. The work was well paid and skilled. A fund was set up to help the now-unemployed staff, and attempts were made to finding them new jobs. The factory was never rebuilt.

Invicta Leather

The works moved to the factory shown in 1901 from elsewhere in Salisbury. Before the Second World War, it had German owners and was called the Colonia Works, but at the outbreak of war the government took ownership and the name was dropped. Once back in private ownership, it was given the name Invicta Works; it ceased trading in the 1970s and was demolished and replaced with housing.

Catherine Street

The corner of New Street, during War Bond Week, 4–9 March 1918. The tank is an early type and was being used to fundraise for the war effort. During the week, it also sat outside the Guildhall, on the Market Square. Note Bonza's Concert Party advertised on the front of the tank, probably a part of the fundraising effort.

Catherine Street
On the right is Larkham & Son Breeches Makers and on the left is Jaeger. An advertising board can be seen halfway down the street for The Palace in Endless Street; one of the shows it is advertising is a benefit, perhaps for the unemployed and/or First World War veterans?

The Canal

Currently known as New Canal. The name originates from the watercourse that ran along here, dug in the early thirteenth century, which drew water from the River Avon. It was also known as the Town Ditch. Rubbish was often deposited in these open water channels in the City, but from 1737 they were realigned and covered over. After 1849, this and other water channels were removed as they had contributed to a cholera epidemic.

The Hall of John Halle

Salisbury is the only place where you may go to the cinema in a medieval building. The surviving hall of the dwelling of medieval merchant John Halle, dating to the mid-fifteenth century, is now the foyer of the Odeon Cinema. Although restored in the nineteenth century, some original features remain.

Charabanc

Popularly used for outings and excursions, they were replaced by motor coaches and buses. Note the speed given under the driver's door: 12mph. The Wheatsheaf pub no longer exists, but the building does. It now houses a jeweller. The advertisement on the side of the wall for Matthews & Co. refers to the Wyke Brewery (Gillingham) founded in 1750, which was acquired by Hall and Woodhouse in 1963. The name of the jeweller now adorns that space. Nutbeem's tobacconist is behind the Wheatsheaf and this may possibly be an outing for Sydney Nutbeem, his staff and families.

Red Lion Hotel

Prior to the eighteenth century, it was known as the White Bear. The range of buildings, containing the carriageway that goes into the well-known courtyard, belongs to the early nineteenth century, but parts of the main building date to the fourteenth century.

Cathedral Hotel
Decked out in its finery to celebrate the wedding of George V. Still operating as a hotel, it is proud of its working Victorian wooden-panelled passenger lift, which guests can use if they wish.

SALISBURY COFFEE PUBLIC HOUSE COMPANY LIMITED.

The Phœnix Coffee Tavern,

29, MILFORD STREET,

❀ **THE ∴ THREE ∴ CUPS,** ❀

SOUTH WESTERN ROAD, FISHERTON (Close to Railway Station).

✎ Comfortable Bed and Sitting Rooms and Good Refreshments at very Moderate Prices. Daily Papers, &c., &c. A Large Room at the Phœnix (will seat 250) for Parties, Meetings and Entertainments.

APPLY TO MANAGERS.

Three Cups Tavern

In 1904, an inquest was held for Ellen Fanny Symes. On 26 April, twenty-eight-year-old Ellen arrived by train and, on enquiry, she was directed to the Three Cups for tea (now an Indian restaurant). Accounts show that, over two to three days, she frequented several drinking establishments with one William Ball, including the Railway Hotel and Engineers Arms, and was drunk for most of the time. Although there was police involvement with regards to her drunkeness, this behaviour does not appear to have been remarkable.

Phoenix Coffee Tavern and Crystal Fountain

Certainly on the evening of 26 April, Ellen and Ball drank in the Crystal Fountain (demolished in 1969) and the Phoenix Coffee House (now Town & Country Furniture). The last that anyone saw of Ellen alive was on the morning of 28 April when she was walking towards Fisherton Mills alone. Her body was discovered in the River Avon some two weeks later at Twenty Hatches near Britford. She was declared to have been 'found drowned'.

Sewell's Milford Street

Called Winchester Street until the sixteenth century, a 1580 survey mentions the 'Catherine Wheel' in Winchester Street, 'otherwise called Milford Street'. Sewell's Stores were housed in Nos 21–23 Milford Street and the proprietor, William Sewell, traded as a pawnbroker and general dealer.

Godolphin School

Founded in 1726 by Elizabeth Godolphin, a Cornish heir, the school opened in 1784 at its first premises in Cathedral Close. It was located in different places in the city over the years, moving to its present site in 1891. In 1898, the fees per term ranged from £4 4s to £6 6s according to age. The Blackledge Theatre has been built on part of the area seen here and is a celebrated venue.

LAVERSTOCK HOUSE
RETREAT

Laverstock House

Originally the seat of the Dyke family, but turned into an asylum by 1754. Advertising as a 'private mental home for ladies and gentlemen', it became quite well known through William Finch's method of treating patients with reason and compassion, rather than the more brutal regimes elsewhere. Two of its more well-known inmates were Thomas Telford Campbell, son of Scottish poet Thomas Campbell, and one of Queen Victoria's 'aspiring suitors'. He was caught within the palace and sent to Laverstock instead of prison.

London Road

No longer London Road, this street was renamed Estcourt Road when the ring road that cuts through Salisbury was built. It was named after Sir Giles Estcourt, 1st Baronet, of St Edmunds College, politician and Royalist.

Greencroft and the Green

Used for recreation, the Green was officially given to the townspeople in 1882. Miraculously, it was little affected by the building of the ring road in the 1960s. It falls within the boundary of the medieval city and was used for some of the five fairs that took place in Salisbury each year in the sixteenth century.

St Edmund's College

Founded in 1269, part of Salisbury's City Ramparts (constructed in 1300–1440) are incorporated into the gardens. It fell into private ownership, eventually being purchased by Rev'd Bourne, who used it as a college and then his private residence. During the First World War, the college was used for quartering officers. Bourne Hill House, as it is now known, has been in local authority hands since 1927.

St Edmunds Church

Bishop Walter de la Wyle founded St Edmund's Church in 1269 but the earliest visible remains are the fifteenth-century nave – there were subsequent alterations to the church up to 1809. The church was deconsecrated in 1973 and in 1975 became an arts centre. In 2003, it underwent a £4.2 million redevelopment, sympathetically changing the character of the interior. It is a flourishing arts centre, with resident artists holding workshops, performances and hosting events for all sections of the community.

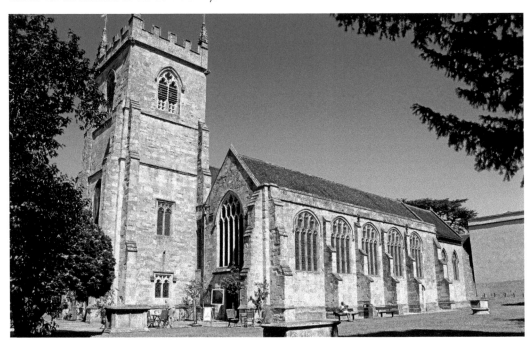

St Edmunds National School

Purpose-built in 1860 near to the church and as a church school. In 1871, elementary education became compulsory for all children and it was one of the largest elementary schools in the city with nearly 500 pupils. In 1927, the same year that the separate South Wilts School for Girls was opened, it was reorganised into a senior school for girls. The present day St Edmund's Girls' School in Laverstock is descended from it.

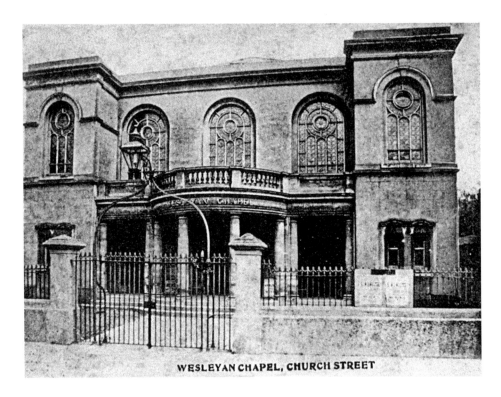

WESLEYAN CHAPEL, CHURCH STREET

Wesleyan Chapel

Salisbury Methodist Church in St Edmund's Church Street (Griffin Chequer). Rev'd John Wesley and eight Salisbury men founded the first church on the site, built in 1759 and leased for 1,000 years at a rent of one peppercorn. The church was demolished in 1810 and rebuilt, then expanded in 1835. Later additions made to the rear were demolished in the 1990s but the façade and main church are mostly that of the 1810–1835 church.

Steam Laundry

Showing the fire of the 19 June 1922. An appeal by a developer against a refusal to allow the raising of the height of the building was dismissed in 2013. Raising the height would have allowed it to be turned into six residential units, but that would have altered the façade.

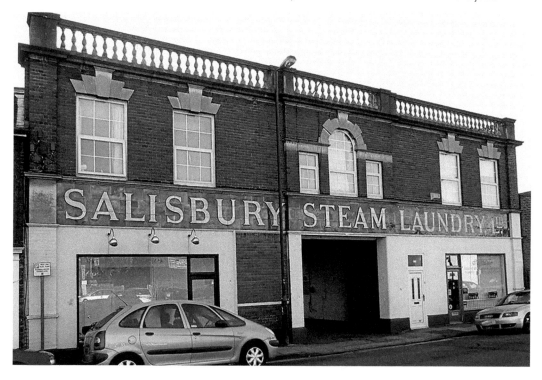

Fire Brigade

Salisbury Volunteer Fire Brigade outside the (now old) fire station, known as the engine house, in Salt Lane. Note the steam rising from behind the firemen, presumably powering the tender. In 1898, Sidney Fawcett was captain and the brigade comprised eighteen men. Fire brigades were very popular; they often put on displays and took part in fairs and county shows. Salisbury Council took over the fire brigade in 1920, and appointed paid firemen.

Endless Street

Showing the Palace on the corner of Chipper Lane. It opened in 1889 as the County Hall and, in 1908, it was the first place to show films in Salisbury. A few years later it was renamed the Palace Theatre but by the early 1930s it had closed. The building has been demolished and replaced with small shop units at street level, with offices above.

Market Square

Our trip around Salisbury brings us back to the Market Square, by Blue Boar Row, looking down to Oatmeal Row and the Cheese Market. It is a hectic, traffic-laden market day, and it is heartening to see that even then, a good photo could be spoiled by scaffolding.

Old Mill in Ford

Run by Edward Griffin for many years as a miller, farmer and dairyman, it is probably his wife Mary standing by the door. By 1911, his son John had taken over all these roles as Edward was in the County Asylum at Devizes. He died in 1912 leaving effects of £3,158 13s and 2d. Outwardly, the mill and its setting seem little changed and it is now a residence, no longer in use as a mill.

Bibliography

A Descriptive and Historical Account of Old and New Sarum, Clapperton, 1834

A History of Salisbury, Dorling, E. E., Nisbet & Co, 1911

Ancient and Historical Monuments in the City of Salisbury Volume 1, Royal Commission on Historical Monuments, HMSO, 1980

Ancient Trade Guilds and Companies of Salisbury, Haskins, Alderman Charles, Bennett Brothers, 1912

Around Salisbury In Old Photographs, Daniels, Peter, Sutton, 1989

Cathedrals of England, Clifton-Taylor, Alec, Thames & Hudson, 1967

City of Salisbury Conservation Area Appraisal and Management Plan, Wiltshire County Council, 2014

Endless Street, Chandler, John, Hobnob Press, 1983

Plain Soldiering, James, NDG, Hobnob Press, 1987

Salisbury Archaeology Survey, Wiltshire County Archaeology Service, 2004

Salisbury Changing City, Purvis, Bruce, Breedon Books, 2003

Salisbury in Detail, Salisbury Civic Society, 2009

Salisbury In Old Photographs, Saunders, Peter, Sutton 1987

Salisbury Past, Newman, Ruth and Howells, Jane, Phillimore, 2001

Salisbury Plain, Daniels, Peter, History Press, 1996

Salisbury, Chandler, John, Sutton 1992

Salisbury, History Around Us, Chandler, John Sutton, 1992

Wiltshire Life and Times, Wiltshire Times, Breedon Books, 2004

www.british-history.ac.uk/

www.britishnewspaperarchive.co.uk/

www.salisburycathedral.org.uk/

www.workhouses.org.uk

www.milfordstreetbridgeproject.org.uk

history.wiltshire.gov.uk/

salisburyinquests.wordpress.com